Sandra's Journey
A Spontaneous Story-Song for Grownup Children

written and illustrated by

Sandra Chausseé

©2010 Sandra Chaussee

All rights reserved. No part of this book may be reproduced or transmitted in any form or by any means, electronic or mechanical, including photocopying, recording, or by any information storage and retrieval system now known or hereafter invented, without written permission from the publisher, except for the inclusion of brief quotations in a review.

ISBN: 978-0-615-41791-2

Illustration and Voice-over by Sandra Chaussee

Cover design and book layout by Amberlee Chaussee

Soundtrack recording and mastering by Jodie Silva

Colorization by Allyssa Power

To purchase additional copies please visit:

http://www.lulu.com/content/paperback-book/sandras-journey/9545957

DEDICATION

I dedicate this book to two of my greatest teachers, Karina Schelde and Eva Goetz. I have them to thank for the "marriage" of sound and story in this book.

Thanks to Karina's sound healing training, I learned to "fly by the seat of my pants". I learned to just "show up"—to trust myself and to trust in the process. This was a big leap for a champion control freak like me. Prior to working with Karina, I was a "paper and pencil" person afraid to face an audience or teach a workshop unless I had reams of written documentation to back me up. But as I began to integrate Karina's teachings, I became more and more comfortable with being myself and with being in the moment. I planned less and experimented more—both with my clients and with my own creative process. As a sound healing practitioner, I'd been using my voice as a healing instrument all along, but because I was also a storyteller, I was curious to know how stories could be used for healing. I knew that a story's "message" was oftentimes healing to a reader but why couldn't the sound, the vibrations, of a storyteller's voice be just as healing? What better way to find out, I thought, than to record my own story-song. I'd been thinking about this for a long time. Then one day Guidance told me that this was the day to sit down with the tape recorder. "Magic" happened that day! As soon as I opened my mouth, I knew that whatever came out was going to come from my heart. It was going to be spontaneous and it was going to evolve from beginning to end without interruption. And so it was that I birthed Sandra's Spontaneous Story-Song in one continuous 90 minute segment! Thank you, Karina!

But that's not all there is to this story. It was Eva who taught me how to give the story its oomph or dramatic effect. Through Eva's Soul Retrieval training and the process of shamanic journeying, I unwittingly stumbled upon the "vehicle" for this book. Sandra's traverse through the "dark night of the soul", her retrieval of the lost pieces of her soul, and her acknowledgment of her gifts and personal power, would unfold as a "journey"—a journey resembling the "dramas" enacted by those of us who participated in Eva's soul retrieval workshop! Through these "dramas" I had learned the value of working with metaphor and symbol and so I knew that it wouldn't be necessary to regurgitate every single detail of my life's story; I could do it more effectively with symbols. When I sat down that day to record and later to illustrate, I was overjoyed that these powerful symbols "magically" emerged! Thank you, Eva!

And so it is with heartfelt gratitude that I thank these two powerful women teachers for sharing their gifts of sound and story with me. I share now the gift of my story with you in the hopes that it will inspire you to grow and to share your story with others. Answer the call! Step into your power! Expand the circle!

Acknowledgments

Daddy
For introducing me to Death at an early age so that I could learn to "father" myself; for the "masculine" traits of Protector, Provider, and Survivor and my logical, practical self

Mama Bird
For teaching me how to "mother" myself; for the "feminine" traits of Caretaker/Nurturer; for the insatiable thirst to become my own person; for the gift of storytelling and child-like humor

Dean
For teaching me that there is "life after divorce" and that in order to gain my life I had to lose it

Andrea Johnson
Daughter, friend and teacher: for accepting me for who I am—warts and all; for supporting those things closest to my heart and soul; and for the vision and entrepreneurial spirit which enabled us to "market a dream"

Amberlee Chaussee
Daughter, kindred spirit and 24-7 technical consultant: for your "bullish" tenacity in "grounding" this work by typing the text, scanning and "cleaning up" the illustrations, creating a mockup, and producing a flawless end product

Bruceau
Soulmate, Seeker, Poet and Philosopher: for the affirmation that life does indeed "begin at forty" and that "the struggle is the goal"; for being my companion on this spiritual quest and for loving me enough to do battle with the dualities of flesh and spirit, freedom and independence, togetherness and solitude; but most of all for teaching me the value of the solitary life

Tulum Sound Sister
For helping me reclaim my birth name, Sandra, and to accept my birthright—the divine child that I AM

Blanca Maria
For the gift of my first and life-long totem animal, Jaguar—the luminous warrior who brought me through the "dark night of the soul"; for teaching me that "invisibility" has its merits and that there's a time to hide and a time to pounce

Medicine Story and Joseph Rael
For welcoming me into the circle of ancestors, storytellers, and sound healers and for helping me to decipher the sounds in my name, Sandra, which means Heaven and Earth

Barbara Flewelling
For turning me on to Deborah Freedman's storytelling class which helped me morph from writing stories on a yellow tablet by hand, to typing them on a computer, to telling them into a tape recorder, to making them up in the moment

Sound Sisters Joa, Barbara, and Mary
For our nights of "spontaneous sounding"; for encouraging me to be "the best me" I can be and for loving me unconditionally when I fall short of the mark

Melissa
For Leapin' Lizards and the spiritual community which helped quench my life-long hunger and thirst for learning; for BOOKS and IDEAS and for the opportunity to grow personally and professionally as a spiritual teacher, healer, and sound practitioner

Jodie
For not throwing in the towel when this project turned out to be more that you bargained for; for your originality, professionalism and insistence on high standards in creating the sound effects, musical background and enhancements for this work and for your patience in navigating the inexplicable key changes and unpredictable rhythms of my voice

Allyssa
For just "happening" to walk into Leapin' Lizards when I was looking for a "colorist"; for loving the tedium of putting color on paper and for the desire to help other people succeed at what they love best

Others
For all those lovers, friends, and acquaintances who "rubbed shoulders" with me on this journey and who contributed to my spiritual growth and development in ways too numerous to mention; for teaching me that there are no mistakes, that there is no right or wrong, but only lessons to be learned

Once upon a time...
when the Moon was silver and the stars glittered in the dark, azure skies... Great Grandmother... rocking in her chair... wrapped in her cloak of wind and stardust and fire in her heart... wild gray hairs flying through the ether... her heart on fire... came... Rocking, rocking, rocking into Be-ing... Sandra.

Sandra, she called,
Sandra, Come forth ...
Sandra ... Great Grandmother calls you, my daughter,
Oh, Great Grandmother calls you, my daughter!
Come forth!
Come forth!

Sandra!
Sandra, you are the stars,
You are the stars, my daughter,
Listen, hear the sparks,
Feel the fire!

Oh, oh, oh...
Hey, hey, hey...
Oh, daughter, come forth.
Reach out your arms and soar through the sky...
Through the sky!
And feel your feet touch the earth.
Grab hold of my ankles,
And I will ground you.

Rock with me, oh daughter,
Rock with me, oh daughter,
Grandmother is singing...
Singing you into Be-ing.

Sandra, you are the heavens,
Of the stars and of the earth,
Heaven and earth you are,
my daughter.

Oh,   S-a-n-d-r-a . . .
These are your sacred sounds.
Sandra... Sandra... Ssss-aa-nnn-d-rr-a.
Sandra, rock with me, oh daughter,
Rock with me, my child,
Rock with me.
Rock with me in harmony.
Rock with me.
Rock with me.
Go with me.
Oh, rock with me.
Oh, rock with me.
Rock with me,
Oh, rock with me...

Oh, rock with me, my daughter,
Rock with me, my daughter,
Rock, oh rock with me.

Rock with me, my daughter,
Rock with me, my daughter.

And Sandra came into Be-ing and she walked the paths of corn, the ones who grew tall and green, the ones of many ears. And in the wind and the land of the plains she grew. And she sat among the silent ones... the ears... and listened.

She listened to hear her song. And she sat among the corn. She listened to the wind and she waited for her time to come...

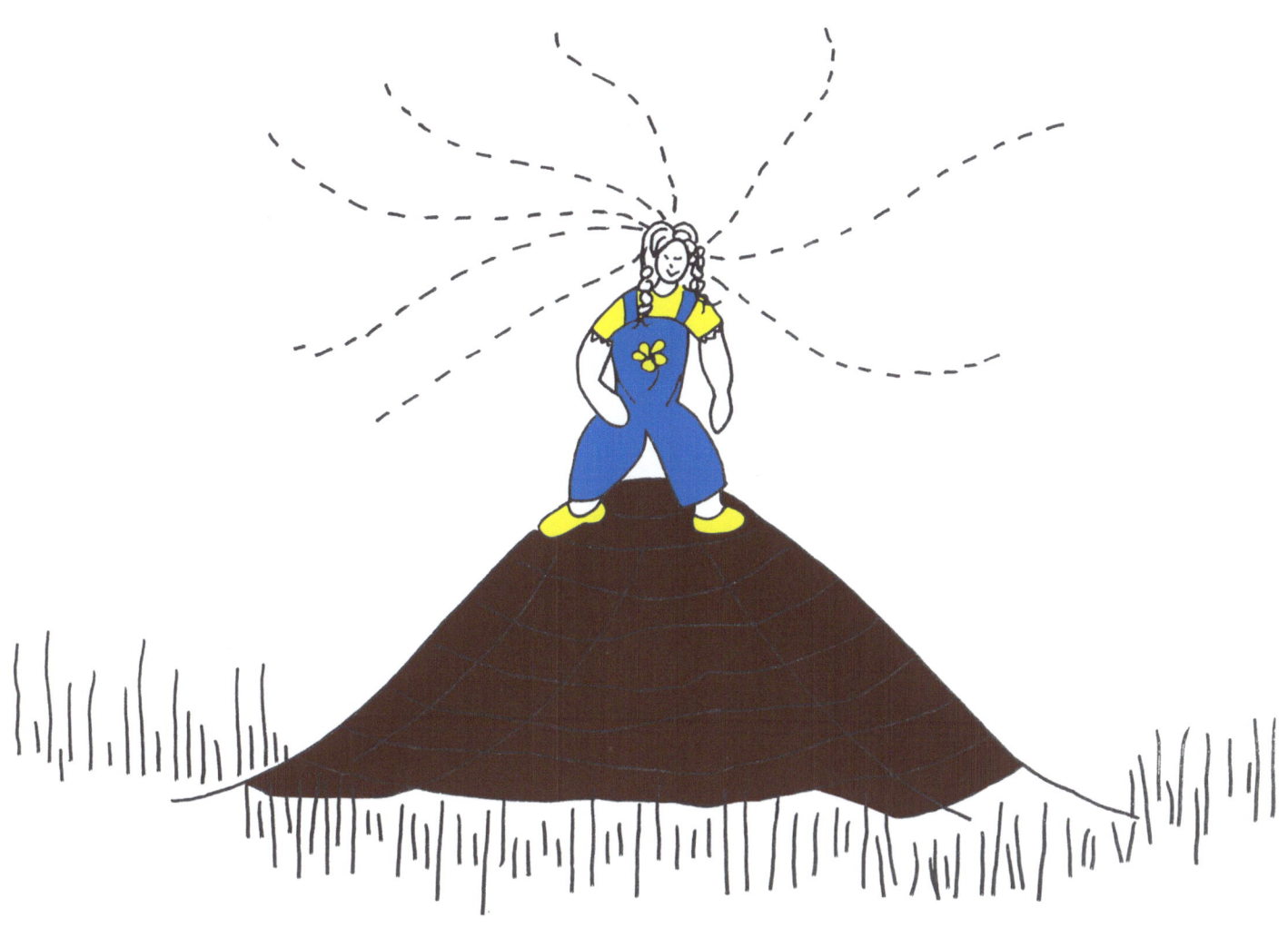

And one day, out upon the land, she found herself on a mound of earth. A little hill, but high to her. Up she went around in a circle. Up she went around in a circle, 'til she reached the top of this round, warm mound. There she stood between Father Sky above and Mother Earth below.

There she stood with the blue of the sky unclouded....
Pastel... pastel... pastel blue and smooth like a sea
surrounding her. Blue, soft blue. Here she could
see in all directions. And her gaze fell upon the land.
Around her, beneath her, surrounding her were...

Sunflowers...

Beautiful sunflowers...
Sunflowers, sunflowers,
Glowing like the fire in the sun.
Yellow... yellow, yellow gold.
Yellow, oh yellow, yellow gold.
Round, oh-oh, golden, golden, golden,
Petals reaching out, radiating light
   from the center,
Petals reaching out...
Radiating... radiating... radiating... radiating
   light...
Light from the core.
Spiraling,
        Spiraling,
                Spiraling,
                        Spiraling...

All the seeds within the intricate pattern,
Round and round and round,
A mandala of light and seeds and yellow,
Yellow, yellow, yellow, yellow in her core.
In her core.
She saw within the sunflower, her core,
The seeds of her Be-coming.

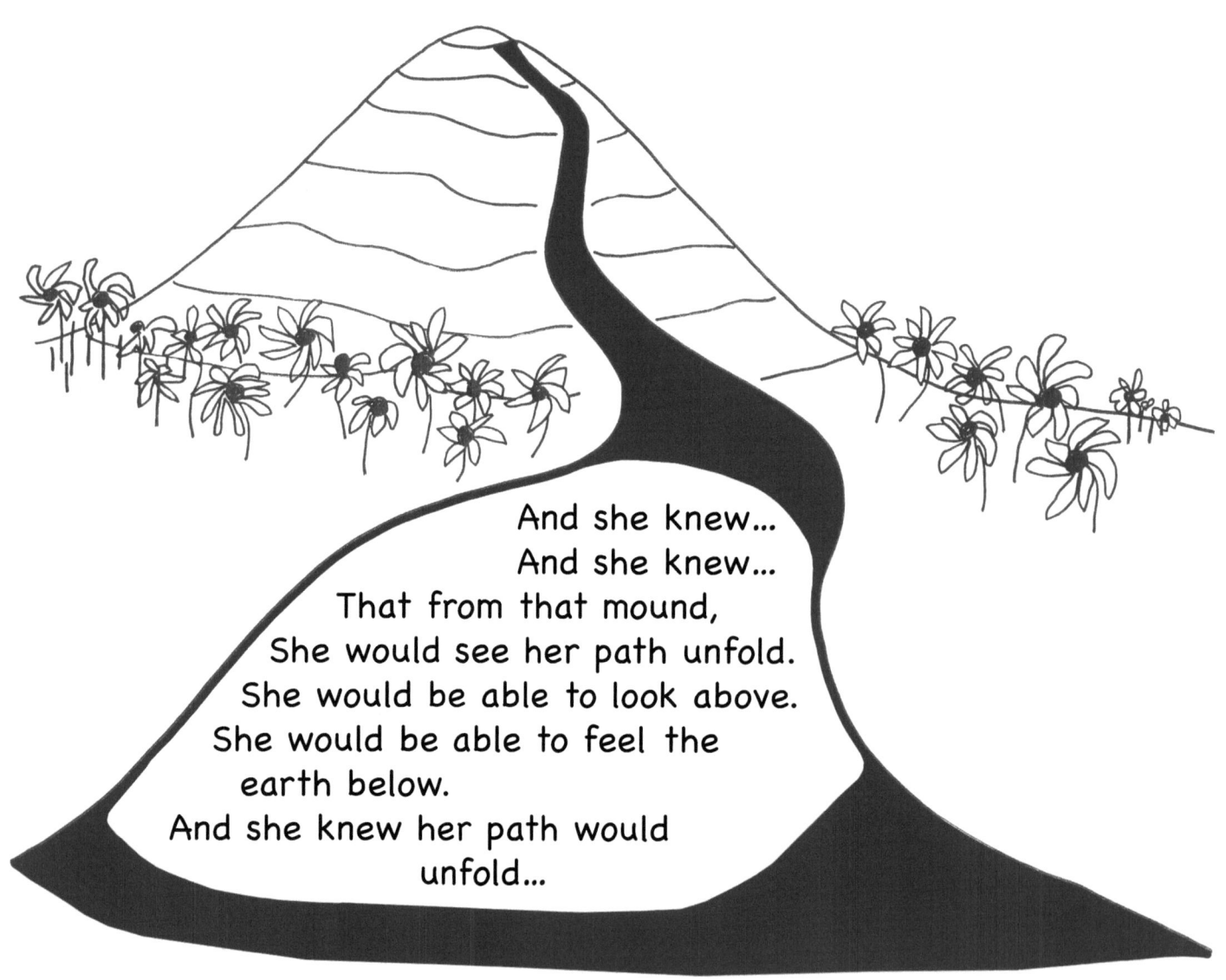

And in her bare feet...
The Barefoot Strawberry Girl, Sandra,
Walked the sandy path...
Feeling her toes in the earth,
Feeling the wind in her hair...

And she walked.
And she grew.
And she walked...

And she dreamed...

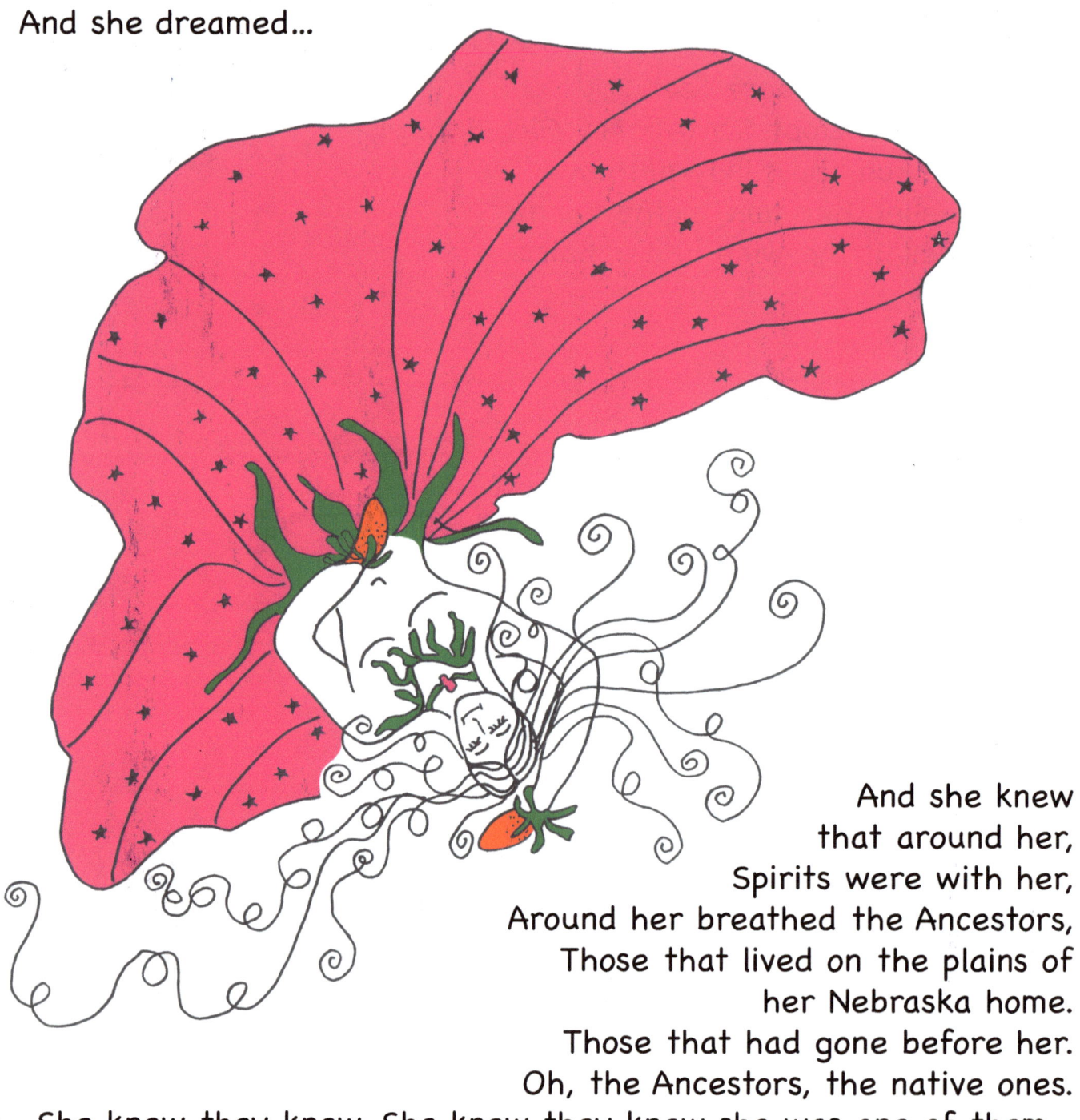

And she knew
that around her,
Spirits were with her,
Around her breathed the Ancestors,
Those that lived on the plains of
her Nebraska home.
Those that had gone before her.
Oh, the Ancestors, the native ones.
She knew they knew. She knew they knew she was one of them...

Remembering the old ways...

Help me to travel between the worlds.
Oh, help me to travel between the worlds.
Show me,
    Show...
        me...
            the...
                way...

The Ancestors heard her calling... and they sent her
                Jaguar...
                Jaguar...
To show her how to tread upon the path...
Steady trail... steady pace... going cautiously but persistently.
      Jaguar, trapper of all trappers.
      The one who knows the darkness...
      The one who knows the silent, velvety blackness
        of the night.
The Jaguar knew the night. Is no stranger to the night...
through the night of the Soul's darkness.
Jaguar...   Call upon Jaguar...

You will be Jaguar Woman...

You ARE JAGUAR WOMAN!

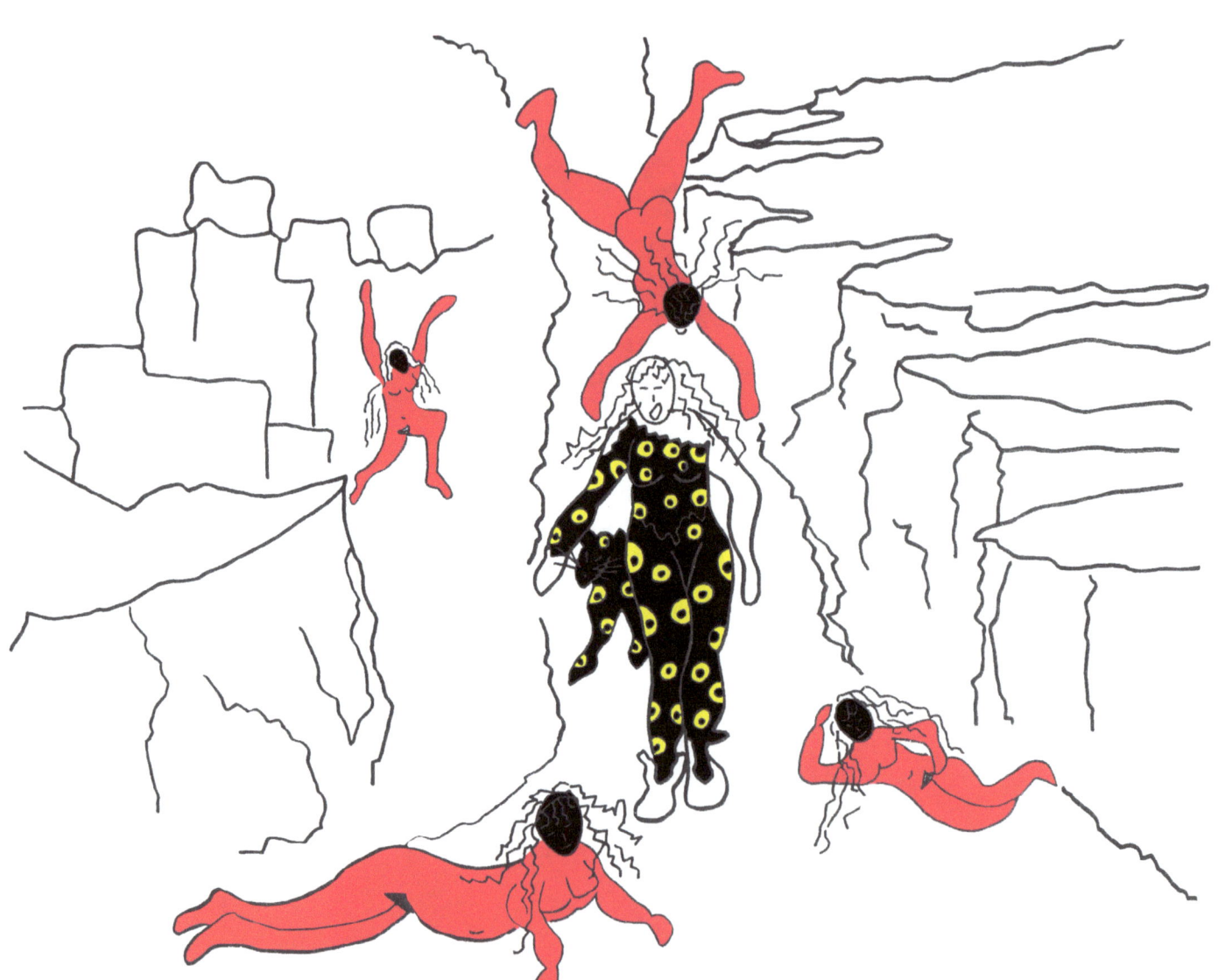

And through the dark nights of the Soul she traveled. She knew the shadows. She knew the demons that lurked within. She befriended them and asked them to reveal to her the lessons she must learn.

Child ...
Wounded Child ...
Ah, ri-ri-eee-ri-aye!
Crying, crying... oh so lost,
Like a mother on the desert floor. In the wilderness,
Crying for her lost child.

Oh child, oh child,
Where is my child?
Ah aye, aye oh... I aye oh hey...
Oh I aye wa ...
Oh child, my child, Oh wounded child,
Oh, where is my child?

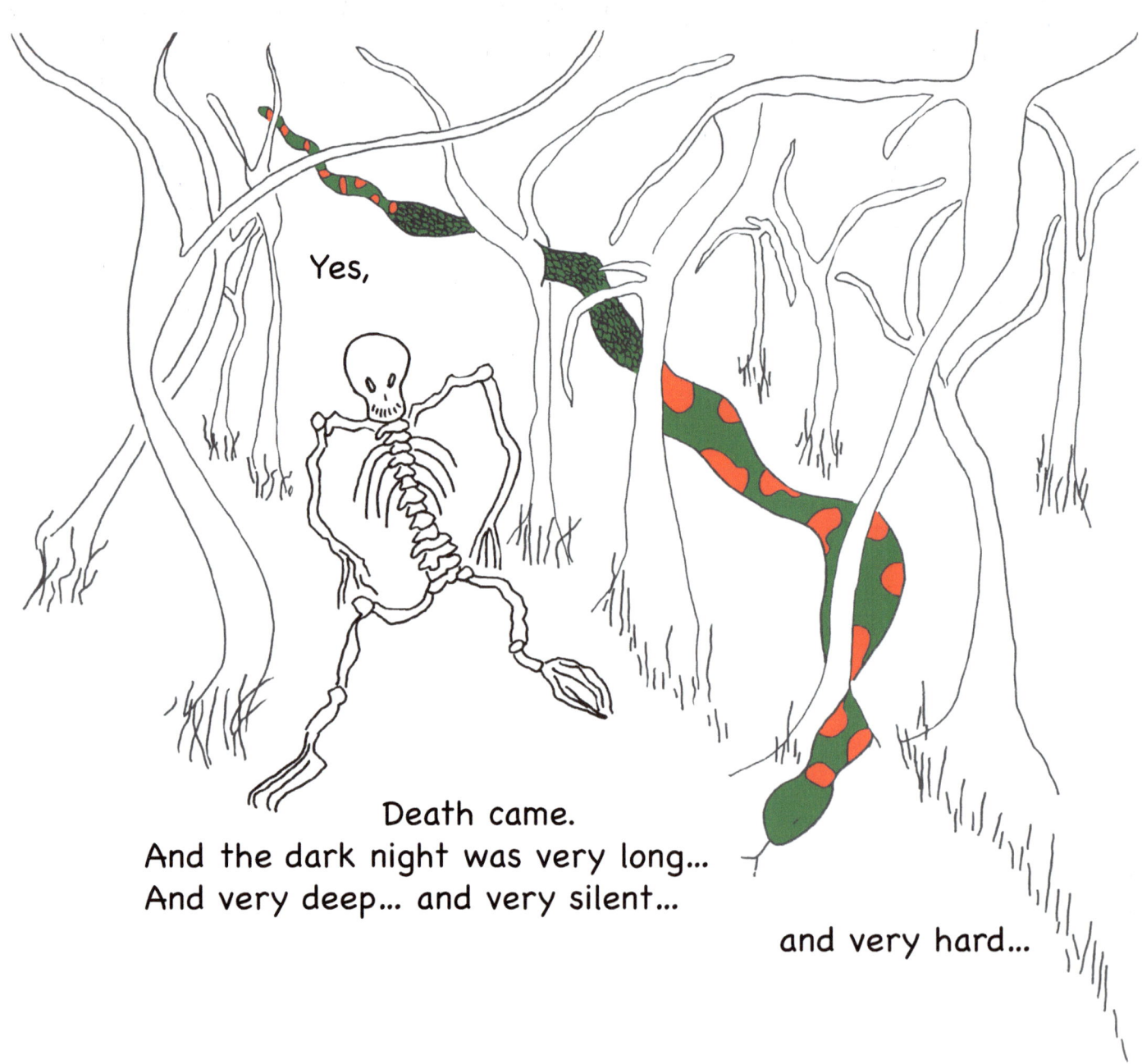

Yes,

Death came.
And the dark night was very long...
And very deep... and very silent...

and very hard...

And it was a long journey.
And it was a hard journey.

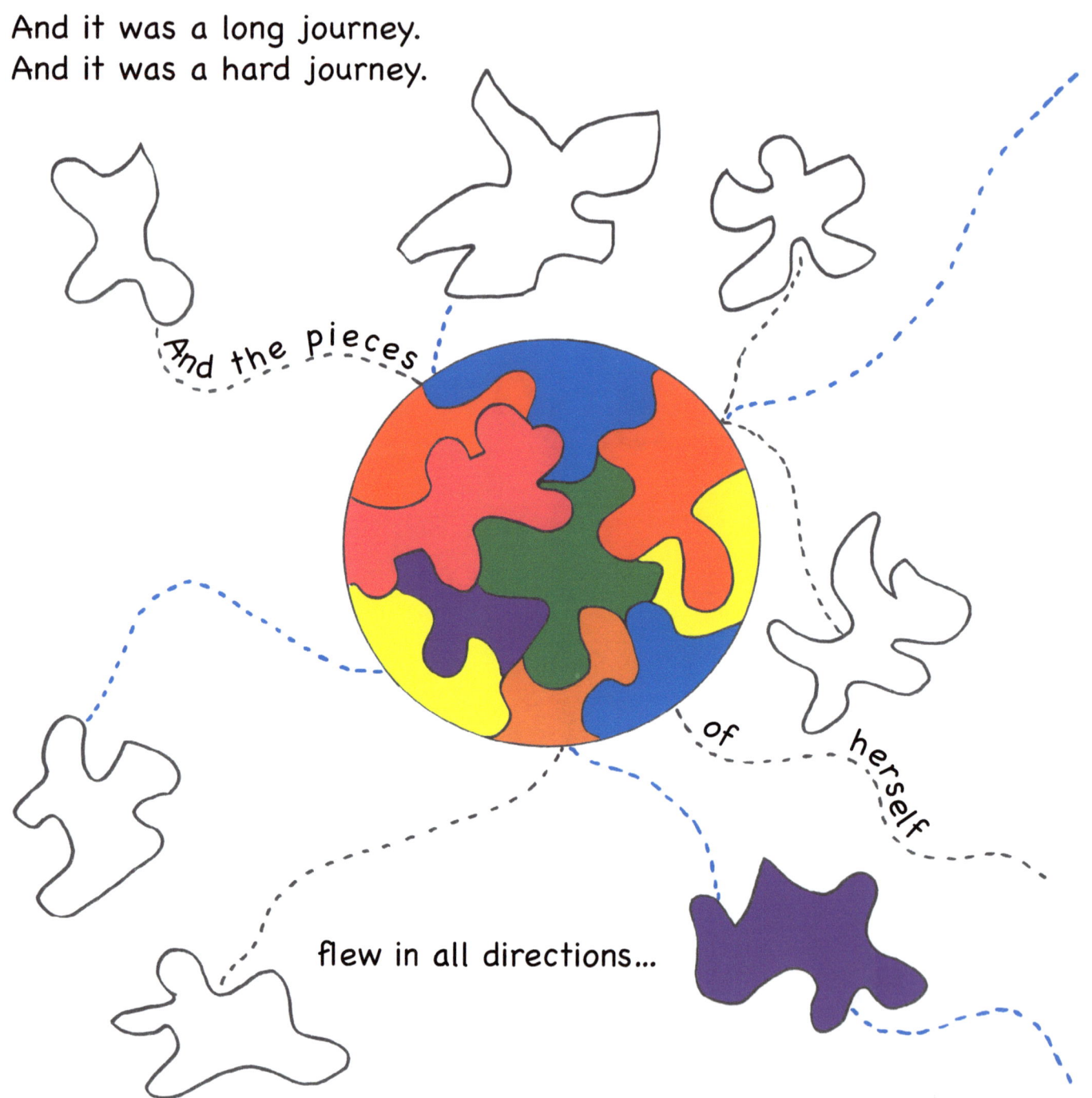

And the pieces of herself flew in all directions...

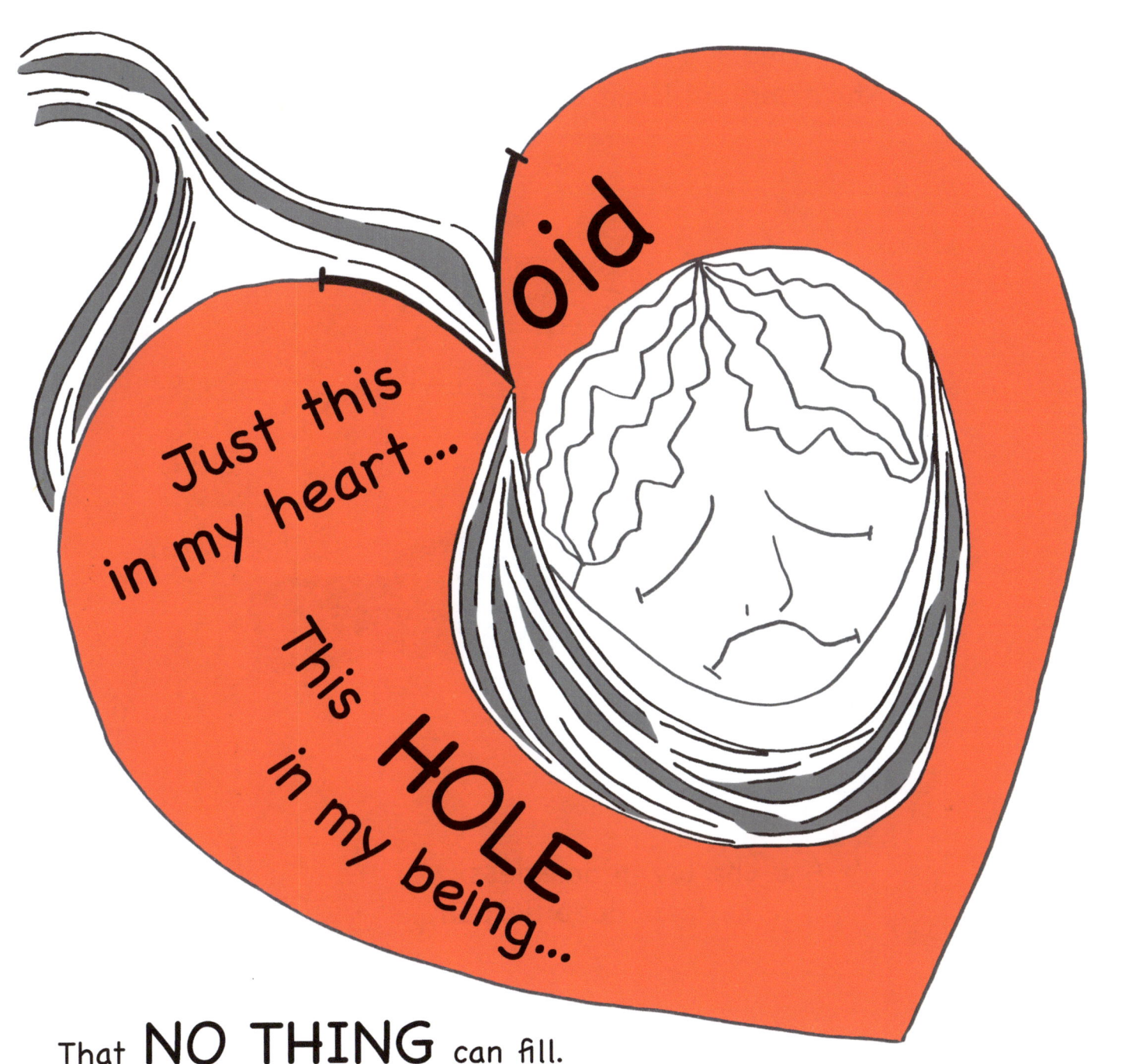

That NO THING can fill.

And so she tried.
And so she tried.
And so she tried until she could try no more.

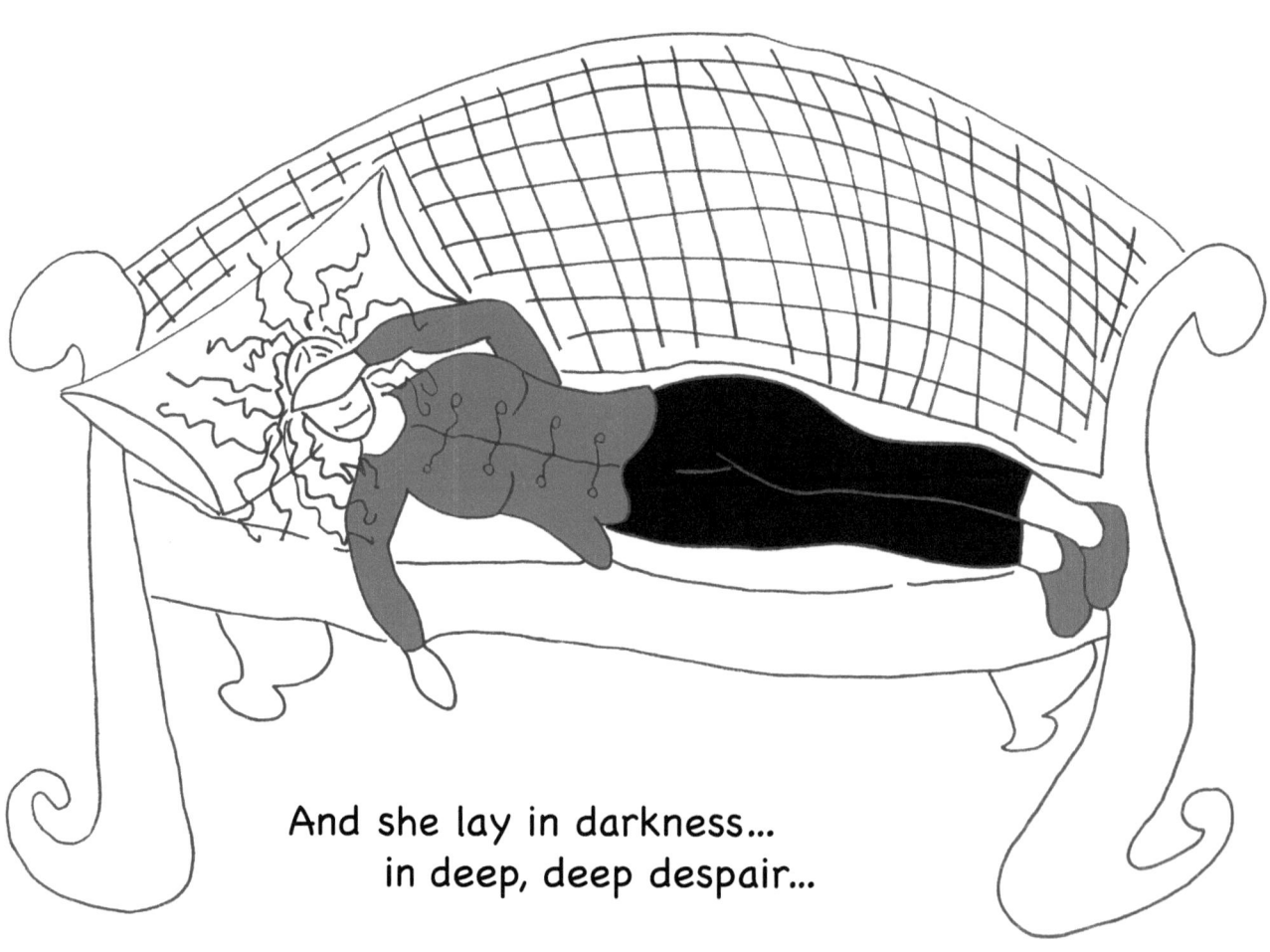

And she lay in darkness...
　　in deep, deep despair...

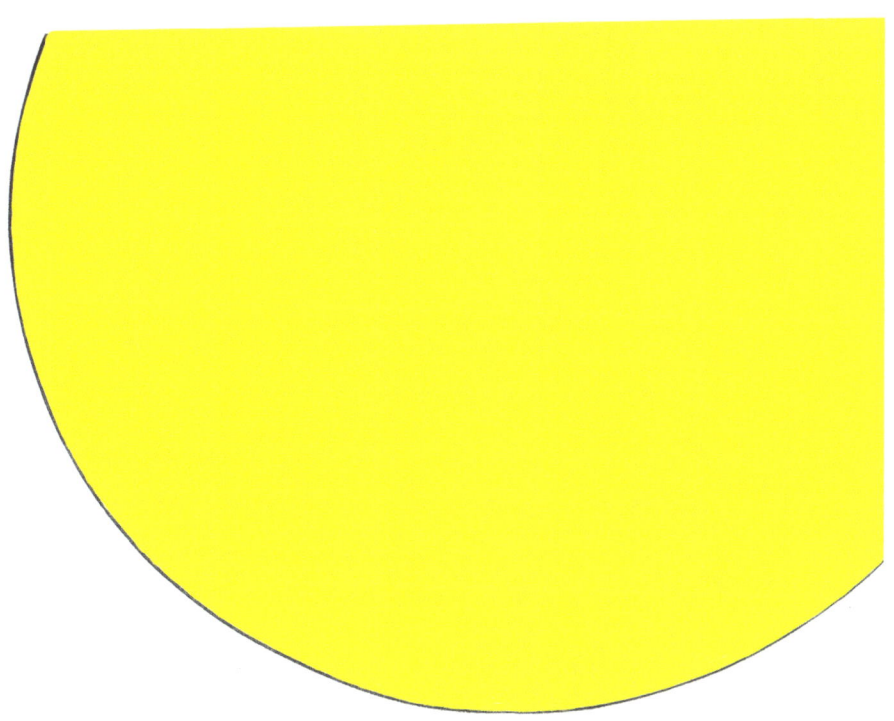

And the Moon shone upon her dejected spirit.
   Oooooo-oooooh-eeeeeeeee-ooo...
Luminescent glow of Moon...
   Moon... shimmering Moon.

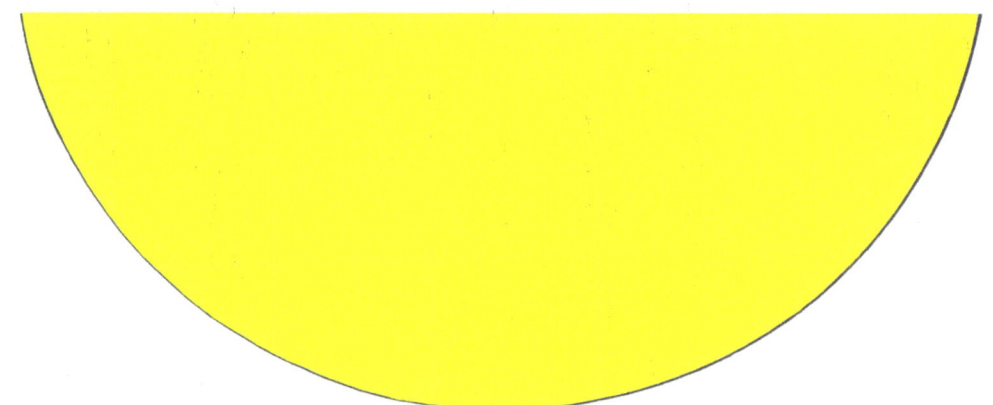

And it shone like stardust on her closed eyelids.
It shone like stardust on her eyelids.

They fluttered.   They fluttered

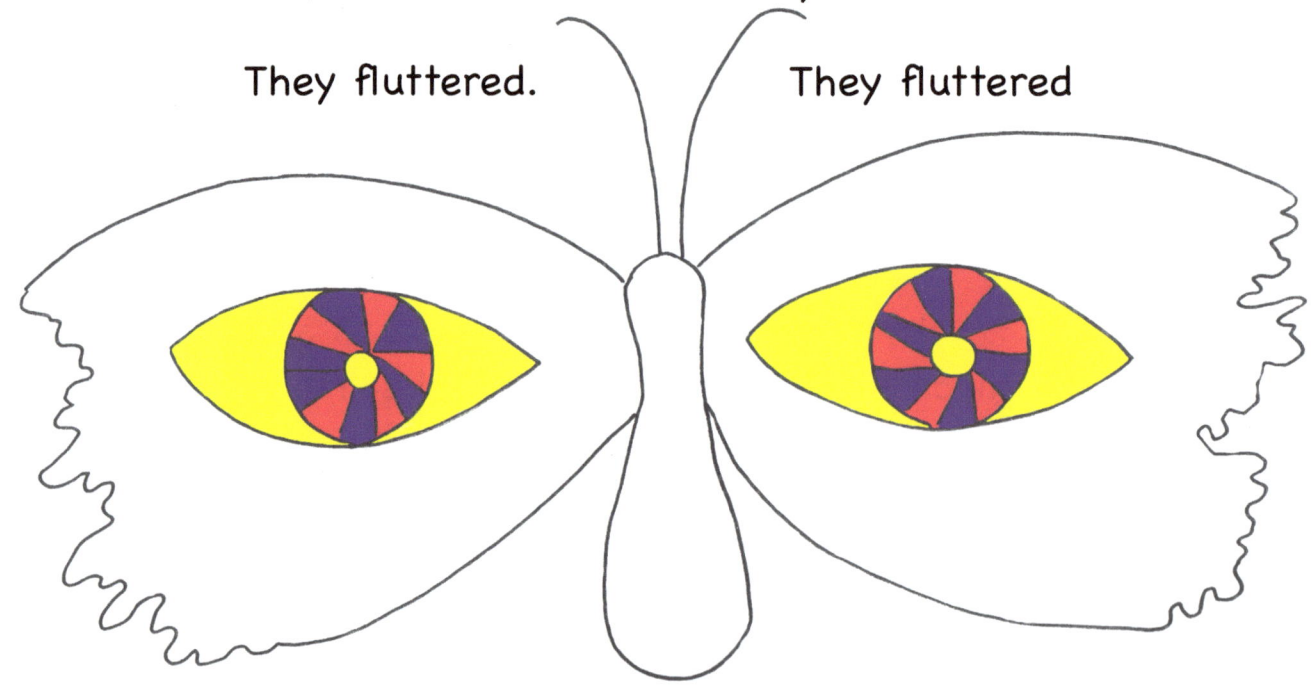

like the luminescent wings of a moth and opened...

And there to her utter dismay and amazement,
She beheld a

SILVER CORD

From her naval
       Spiraling...
               Spiraling...
Out to the far reaches of the Universe
    and beyond...
To the Source of All Creation...
To the Source of All Creation...

A   SILVER CORD...

She knew not what it was or what it meant.
She had no acquaintance with mystical things.

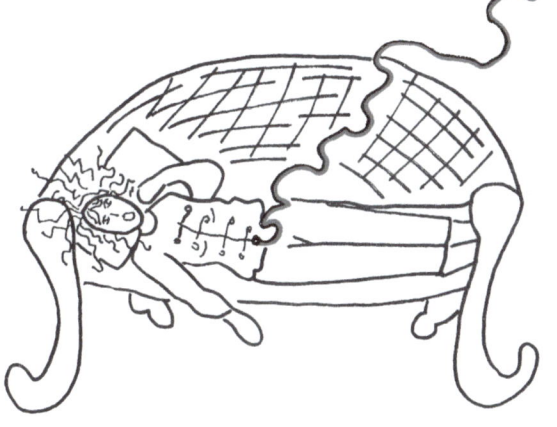

She knew no magic.
She was no sorcerer.

She knew only the cord and the
dark land she was in...

                                 but then...

but then...

There was this **SILVER CORD**
That seemed to be saying to her spirit...
to her soul...

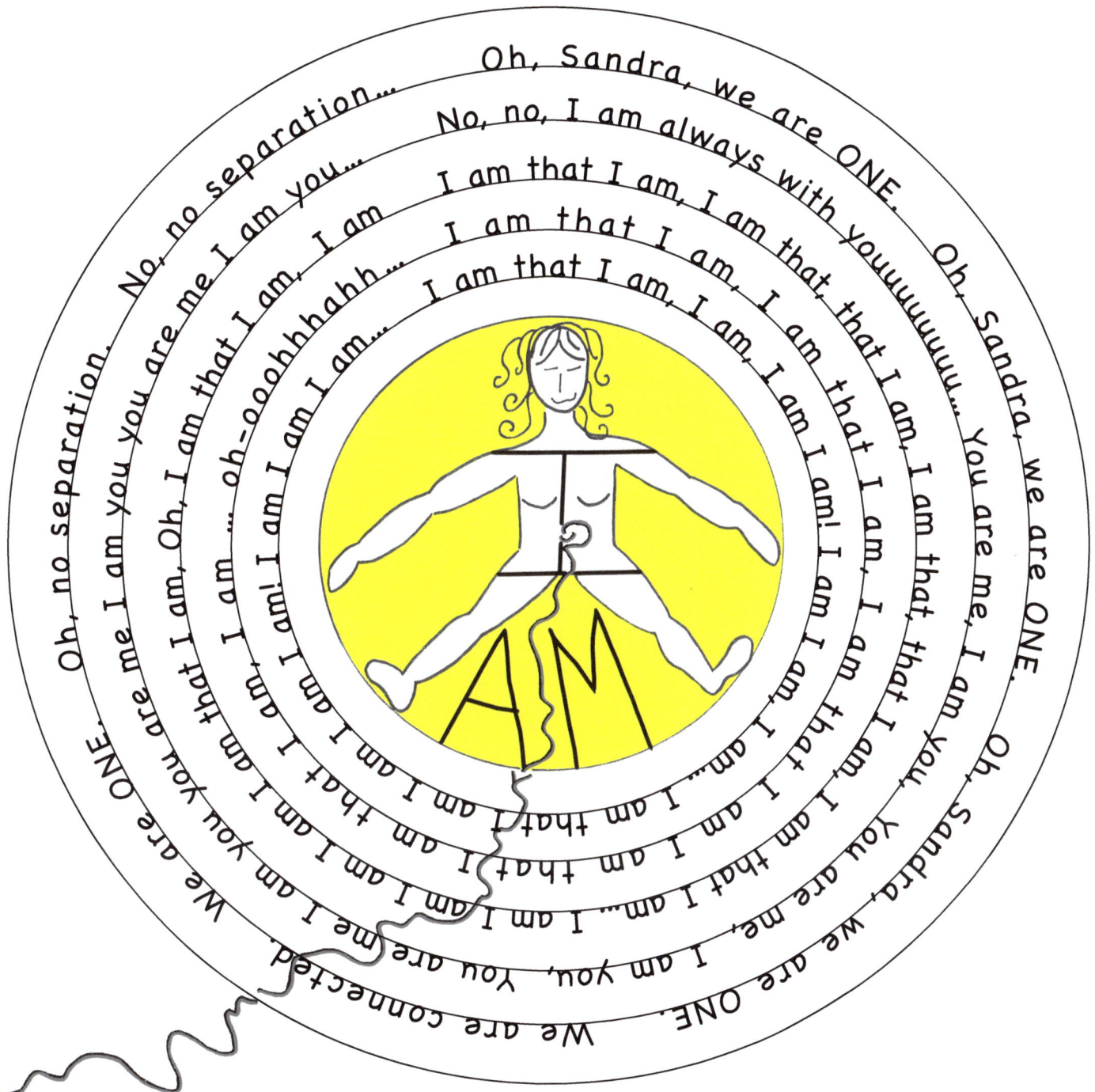

And the lost child, the young maiden, rose from her deathbed... rose from her couch... rose and walked again.... And the maiden wandered the land in search of herSelf.

Where must I go? she asked.
What must I do? she asked.
Who do I talk to?
Where do I go?
Where is my map?

What
do
I
do?

Who will take me there?
I've lost my way.
What direction do I go?
How do I find mySelf?

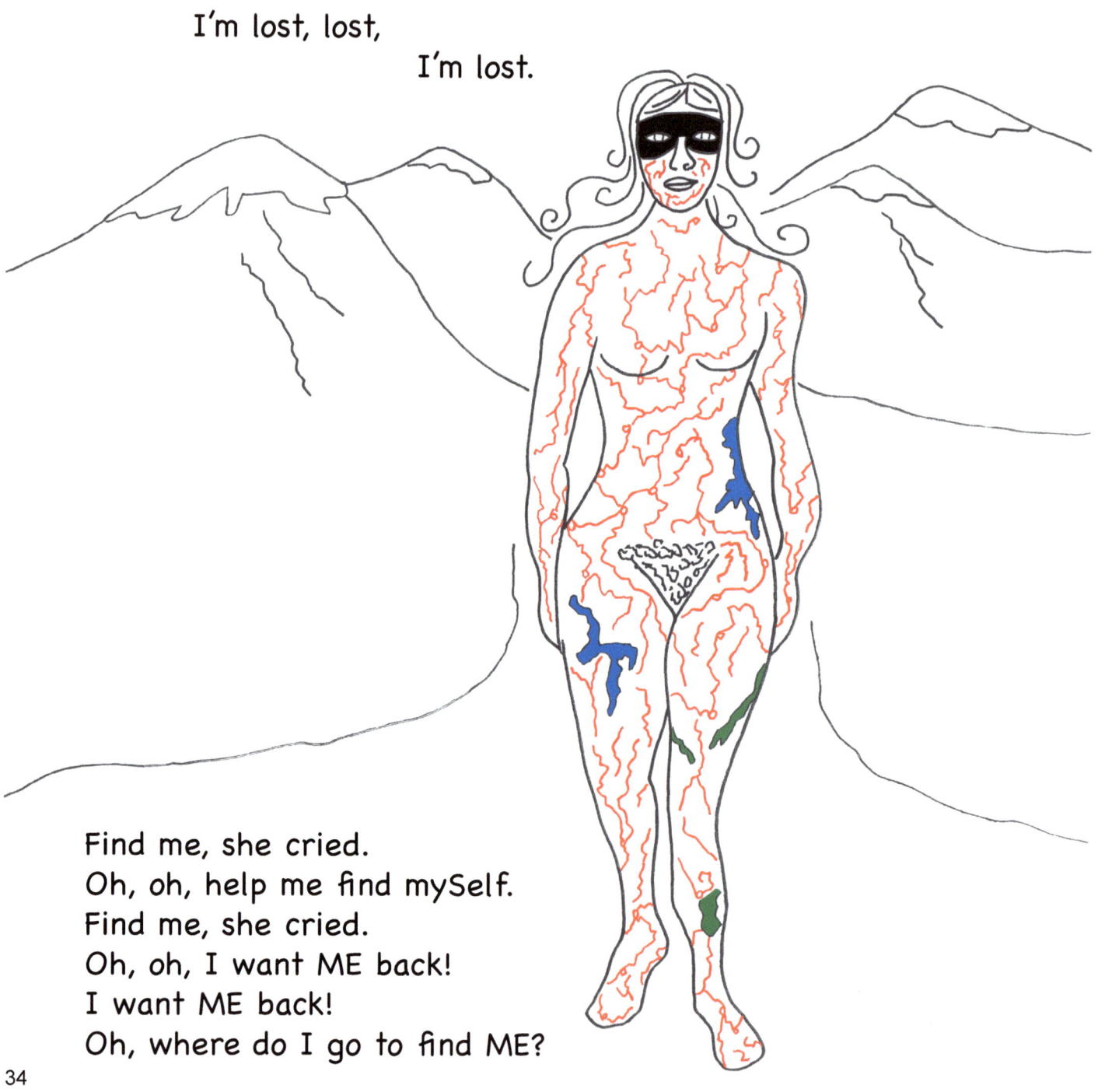

I don't know who I AM!

And from the sky
    one day there came
A winged messenger
With wide-spread wings
    And sharpened eye
Who could see in all directions
            with
                CLARITY.

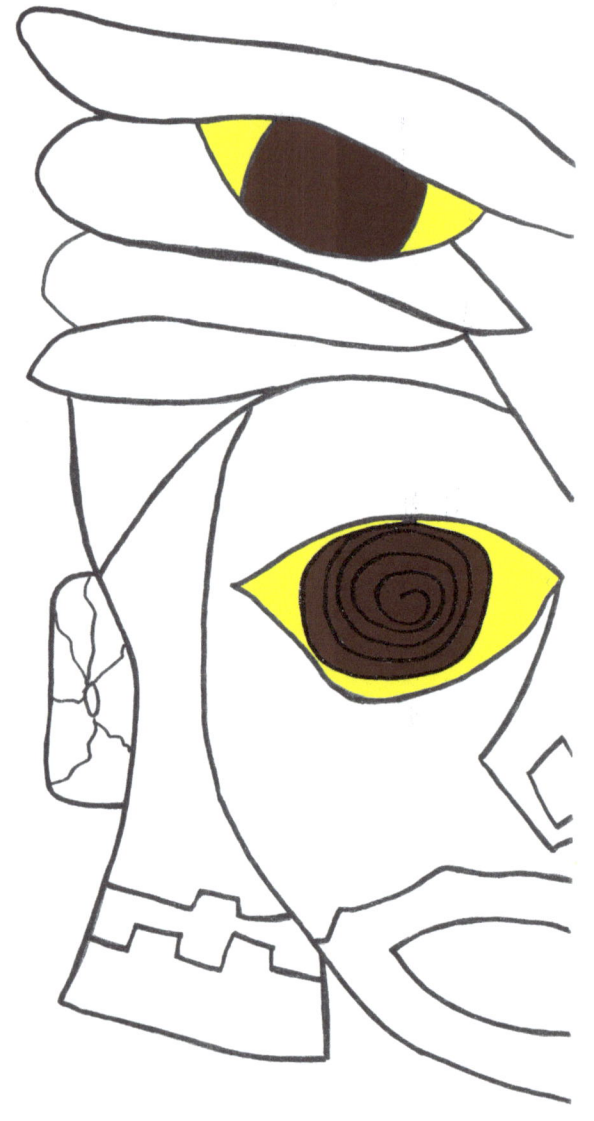

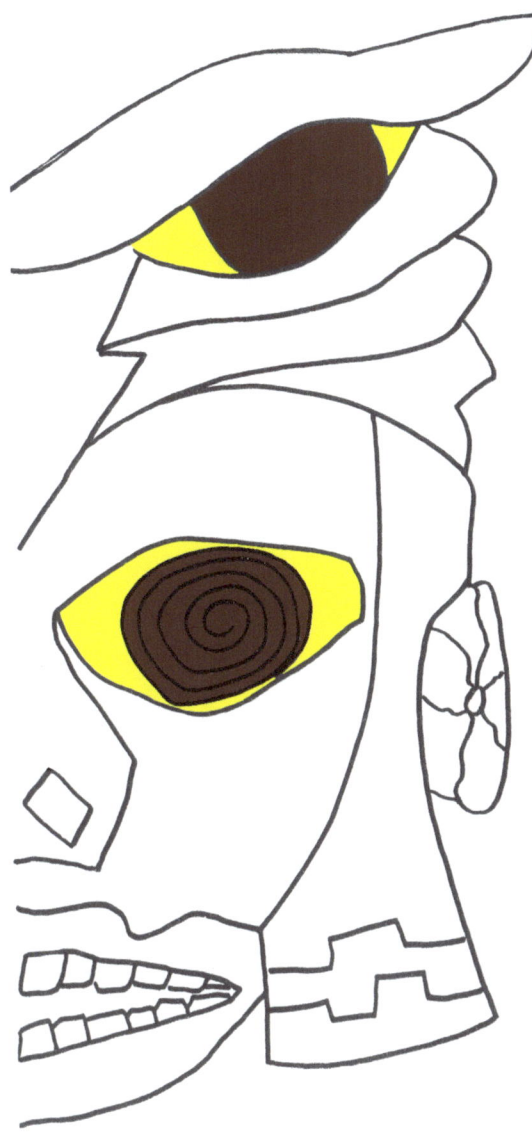

And the winged one
Saw her pain...

And

S
 w
  o
   o
    p
   e
  d

Into her midst and landed into her vision...
And stared deep within the maiden's eyes
And said...

Daughter! Daughter!
Stop this nonsense!
Spider Woman has you in her web...

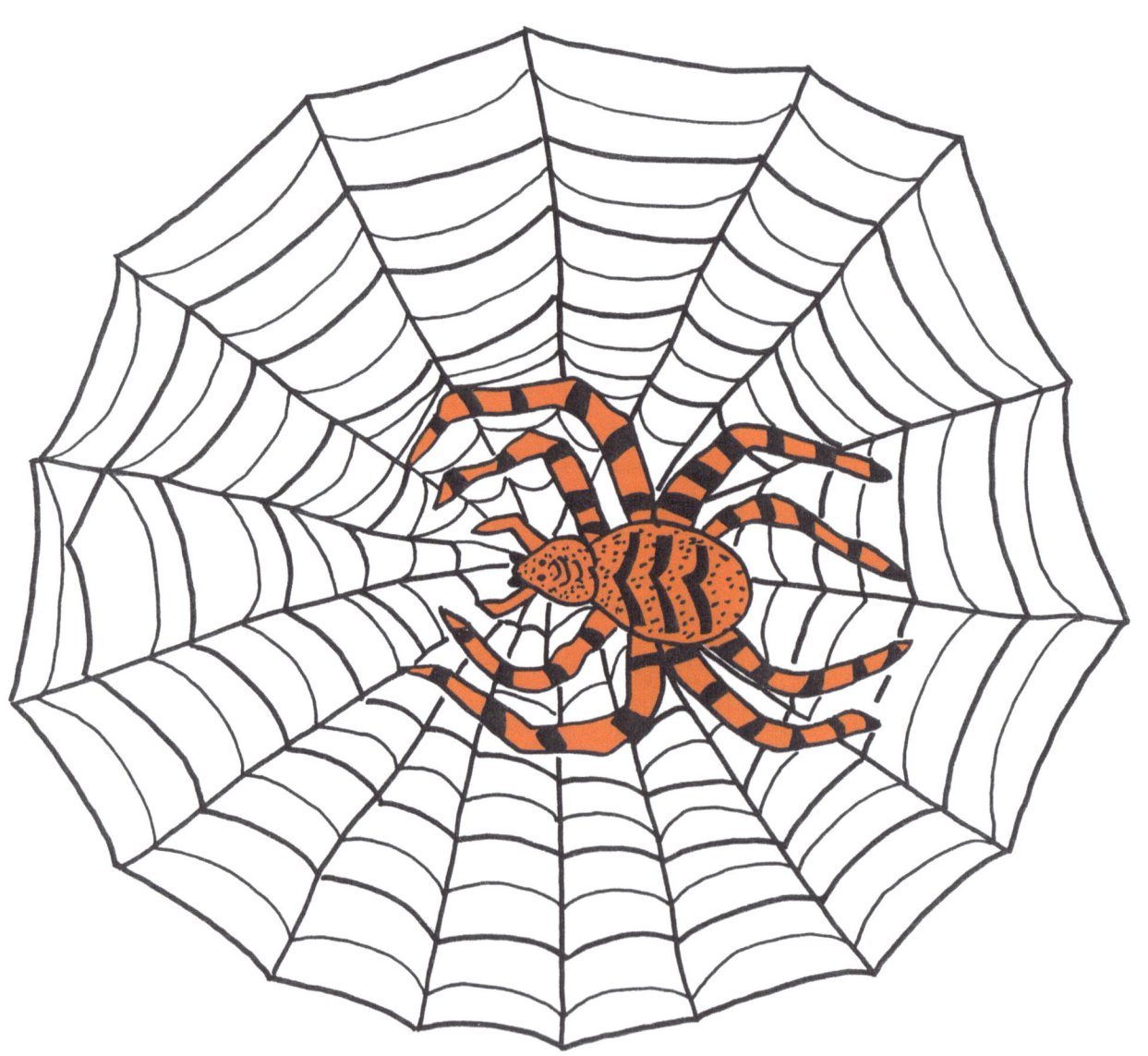

And if you get too far within its center,
Too entangled in the web of all this illusion...
If you get caught in it... attached to it,
You cannot SEE.

You need to find your way to the periphery...
    The outer edges...
Climb out of the web,
   Climb out to the outside of the web
Where you can breathe and see the OVERVIEW again.

Oh, Daughter,

Do not entangle yourself within the web of your life,
        It's only a gossamer thread...
        Instead...
        Daughter,
        Climb on my back and soar with me!
        Oh, come with me and see
        What you were meant to be!

Oh, Daughter,
I have the vision of your HIGHEST SELF within
My breast... underneath my feathers,
Oh, climb with me to the mountain,
Climb with me to the summit.

Oh, come with me.
Oh, climb with me.
Oh, be who you were meant to be.
Come into BE-ing.

Come with me,
Oh, come into BE-ing,
Come into BE-ing,
Come with me.
Come with me and come with me and come and come into BE-ing.
I will teach you to soar...
                       soar...
                                soar!

Come with me.
Come with me.

And so the maiden heard the Eagle's call.
  It was clear and concise.
    And she knew to find herself
      She must soar to the far reaches of the Universe.

So she climbed on the Eagle's back,
    And with her she took from her native land,
  The basket that Grandmother had woven her long ago.

And she listened to the echoes of her Grandmother's words...

Daughter,

Rock with me,
Oh, Daughter, rock with me,
Oh, Daughter...
Rock on, rock on, rock on...
Take with you, my Daughter,
This basket I have woven from the sweet,
sweet grasses of your native land of Nebraska...

Take with you, my Daughter,
These weavings of the basket,
These weavings of your life...
These weavings like the braids, the sweet braids, of your hair.

    Take this basket, Daughter,
    Take this basket, Daughter of the Land,
    And gather yourSelf together,
    Gather yourSelf together.

Go, my Daughter,
Go and reclaim all those scattered, scattered sands of your soul,
    Put them in the basket, Daughter,
    Put them in the basket, Daughter,
    Put them in the basket, Daughter.
Make yourSelf WHOLE.

    And so the maiden listened,
      She had with her the sweet basket
    Gifted to her by Great Grandmother...
    And she climbed upon Eagle's back,
      And she tucked her toes
        beneath Eagle's wing,

And she took flight with Eagle in search of her fragmented soul...

Heh-hey-oh-hi-weh-ha...
Heh-hoh-hey-a-hey-a...
                    And so it was a gentle flight

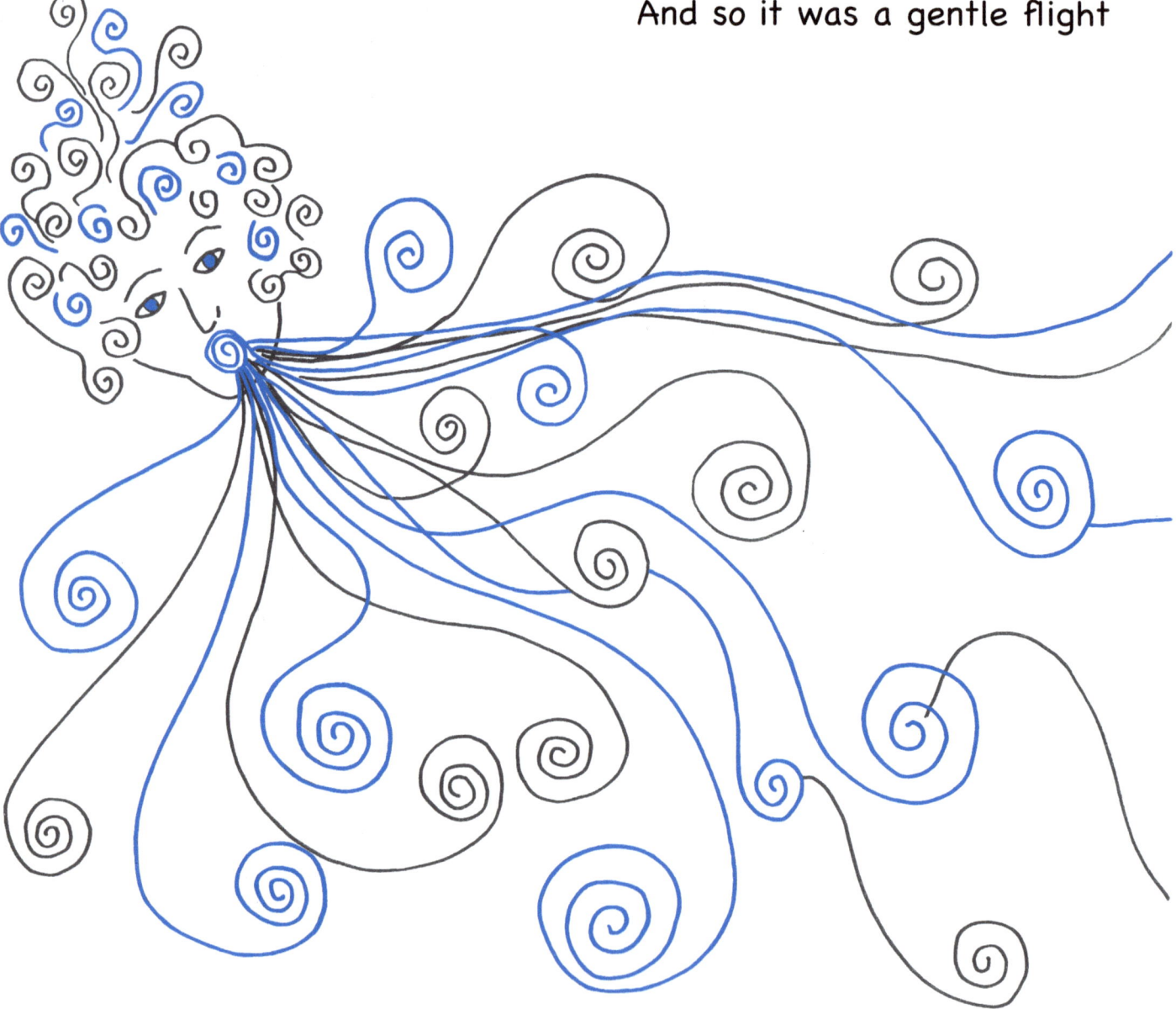

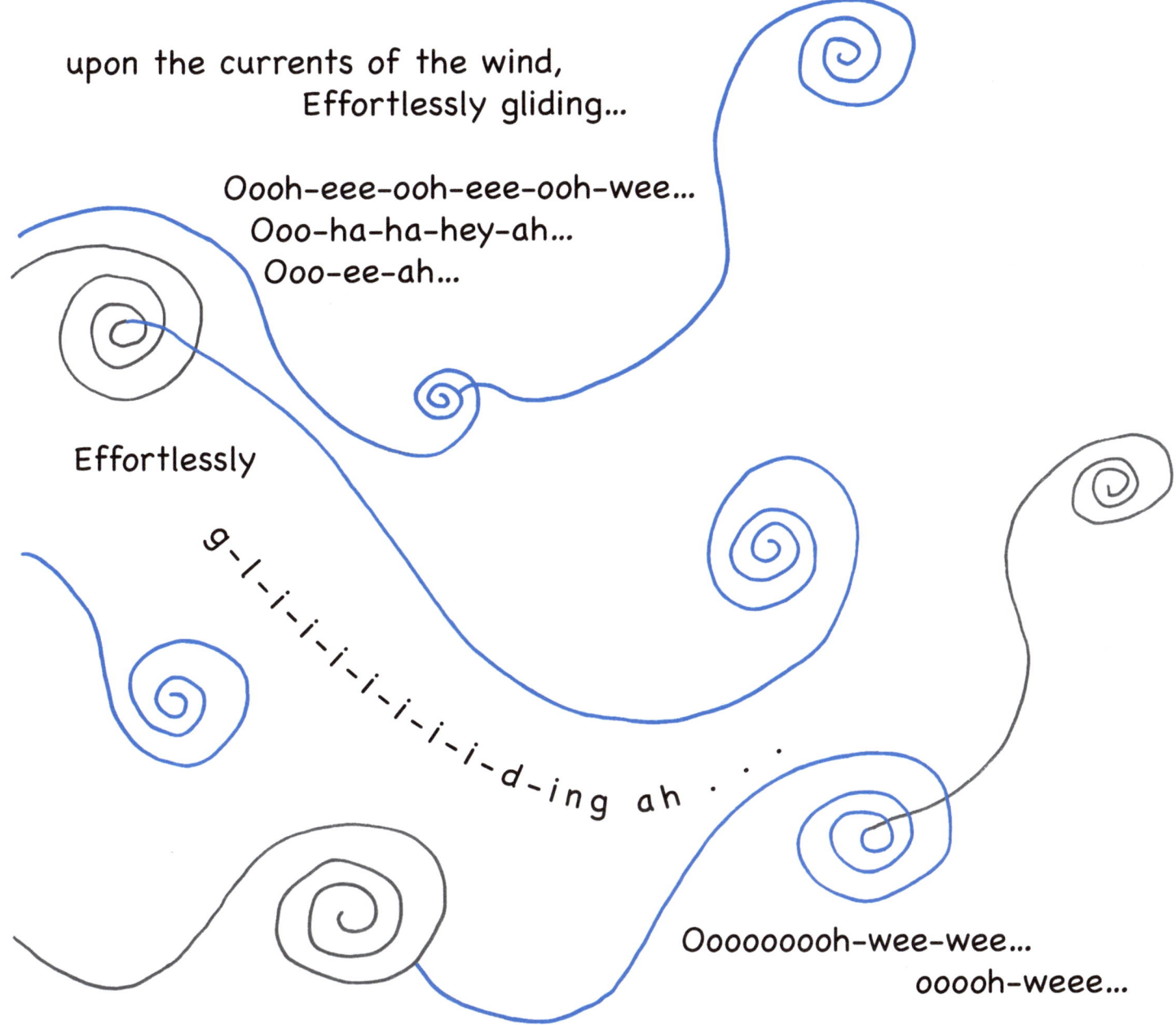

upon the currents of the wind,
        Effortlessly gliding...

    Oooh-eee-ooh-eee-ooh-wee...
    Ooo-ha-ha-hey-ah...
    Ooo-ee-ah...

Effortlessly

g-l-i-i-i-i-i-i-d-ing ah . . .

          Ooooooooh-wee-wee...
                ooooh-weee...

And as the maiden glided through the air on Eagle's back,
she could see the demarcations in the land below her as if her whole life was laid out upon the Earth's surface.

There were peaks of mountaintops.
There were valleys.
There were rocks and barren places... and deserts.
There were flowing rivers...
All these things.

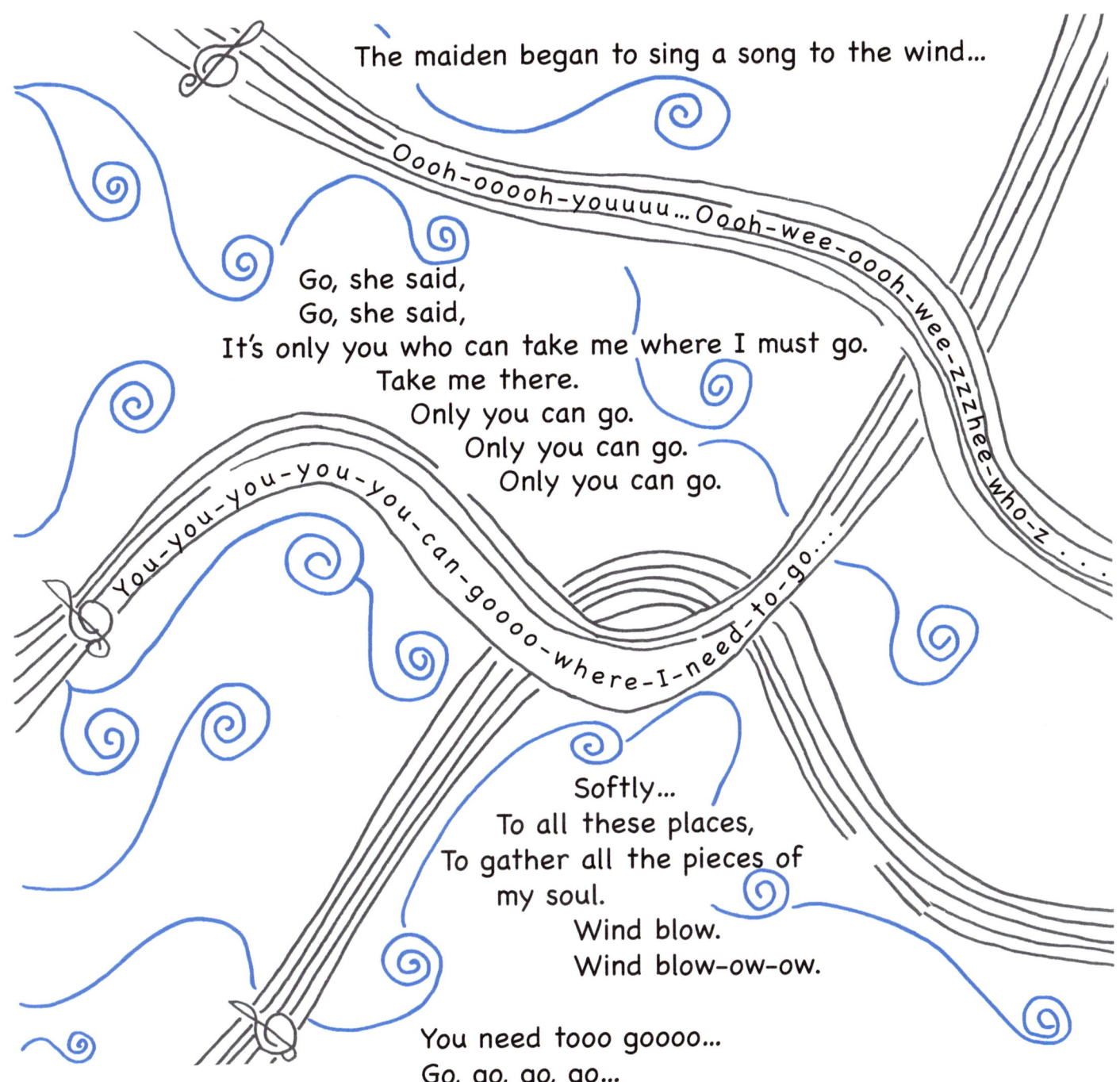

And Eagle was so happy with his passenger on his back,
He flew, he flew into the Sun...
Flew across the mountaintops.

He soared higher...
and higher...
and higher...

And he took her even higher.

How high Eagle you fly!

The maiden thought, Oh, I cannot go higher...

And as they continued to find their way to other realities
and dimensions and worlds unknown...
There the maiden began to see

crystals

and colors

and lights

and sounds

and things beyond all imagination,
sparkling at her
like the twinkling
of the stars...

Diamonds,
Diamonds of her soul...
The facets of all that she is ...

And she began to see as if in a diamond, multifaceted...
That she had her own beauty and uniqueness and gifts...

Sparkling like diamonds...
Flowing from her like the sparkling crystal waters of mountains and glaciers.

CREATIVITY sparkling!
Diamonds!
FIRE!
PASSION!
ENTHUSIASM!

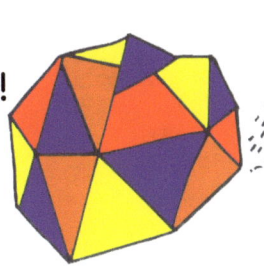

Wisdom of the Ancestors,
Ancient teachings.
Yes!
Yes!
These were her GIFTS!

And the maiden wondered...
Oh,
oh, oh,
oh,

What am I to do with
these gifts?
Oh, oh, oh, oh...
What am I to do with
these sparkling stars...
these diamonds...

these facets of mySelf?

And then Great Grandmother's voice came to her clearly again...

Oh, Daughter,
Oh, Daughter,
Oh, Daughter,

Gather these stars around you...

The diamonds shining...
And wear them like a cloak,

A shawl around your shoulders.

Oh Daughter, wear them, keep them close.

These are your gifts.

Oh, wear them, Daughter,
    With pride and also humility,
Honoring yourSelf and Great Spirit
    As you use them for good,
    As you use them to serve.

Wear them,
    Gather them,
Put them around your shoulders,
Wear them,
    Gather them,
Put them around your shoulders.

They are your gifts.
They are your unique gifts.
They are your POWER.

Know, my Daughter,
    These are Creator's gifts to you.
    They are your POWER and
        you must wear them.
    You must wear them,
    Wear them, wear them, well.
    Wear them, wear them, well.

To honor both yourSelf and
    your Creator.

And so the maiden gathered the stars,
    gathered the diamonds,
      the facets of her many selves,
And put them around her shoulders like a shawl
    to be worn with dignity and honor ...
And a soft, but powerful, cloak of POWER.

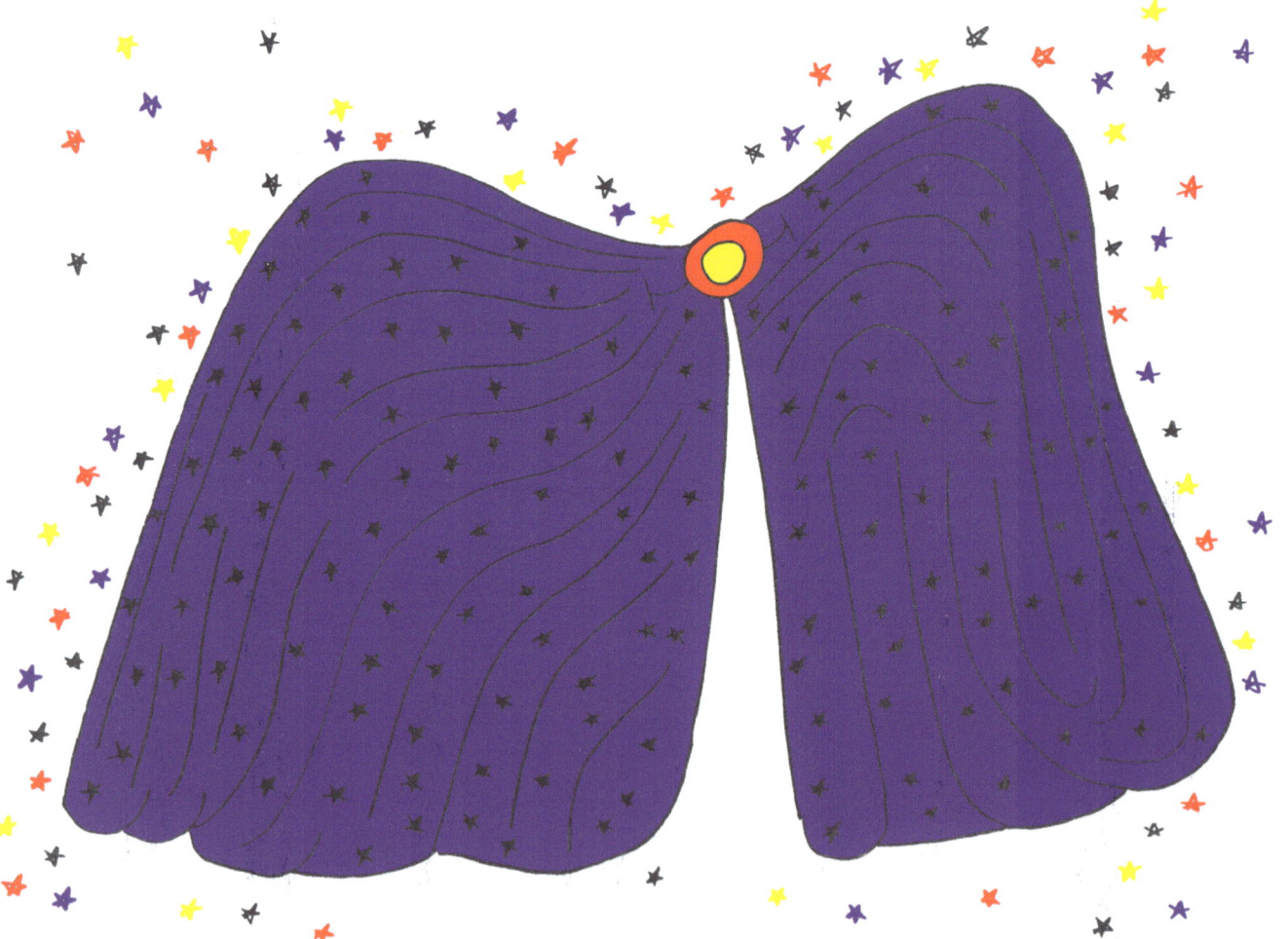

Oh, oh, oh, oh, oh, oh,
Oh, Eagle, my friend and teacher,
Great Winged One,
I do not want to leave the strong back of you,
I do not want to leave.
I want to plant my feet, my toes,
    beneath your wings forever.
I want to stay in this land of SOARING!

    I DO NOT WANT TO LEAVE!
Oh, I do not want to go.
Do not make me go.
Oh, Eagle ...
Oh, Eagle ...
Oh, Eagle ...
Oh-oh-oh-oh
Do not make me, make me, make me go!

Eagle said,
    But my Daughter,
    My Sister,
My beautiful Maiden One,

                    It does not mean that you can never return
    to this land, this place,   this OTHER...
It is always with you.
But you have work to do,
    my Daughter,
You have work to do,
    my Daughter.

Hear the Ancestors call you.
Hear the Ancestors calling...
Oh oh...
Hear them.

The Wind...
It's only the wind, she said.
Only the wind,
It's only the wind,
    My Brother, the wind.
It's only my Brother, the wind,
  It's only the wind,
    It's only the...

my Brother,

Oooooh
  ooooh
    ooooh
      ooooh...

No, my Daughter,
It's not the Wind.
It is not the wind.
Listen again...

 It is, it is the voice,
      the voice of your Ancestors.
Calling,
Calling you Home,
To return again Home.

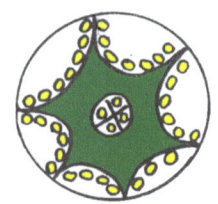 Calling,
Calling you...
Oh-oh-oh-oh you...

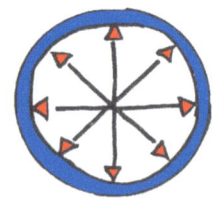  

Yes, my Daughter,
We are all ONE.
We are all the voices within you
    calling you HOME.
Join us in the Sacred Circle, Daughter,
We are calling you HOME.

You must join us now.
You are one of us now.
You are to take your place
    within the Circle,
Bringing us honor,
Honoring Great Spirit with your gifts,
Stepping into your power and your purpose.
Be-ing ON PURPOSE.
Come with us now.

Hey-hey-hey-wah
Wuh-ya-hey-a
Wa-ya-hey-ohey
Hoa-hoa-hey

Take this wand,
> Oh, take this magic wand,
> Take this wand.
> It is the wand of Spirit talking.

Oh, oh, take it now.
It is your fire.
It is your fire.
It is your Shaman's fire!

> Oh, ignite the hearts of others,
> Help them to burn brightly as the stars.
> Oh, ignite their fire.
> Oh, ignite their fire.
> Oh, be the Shaman with the wand of fire.

Oh, answer, Sister,
Answer, Daughter,
Answer, Granddaughter.
    Answer the call.
    Answer the call.
    Answer the call.
Come and join the Circle.
Come and join the Circle.
Answer the Ancestors now.
Answer the Ancestors now.

Calling... calling...
    Calling you... HOME.

And so the maiden who was now in her full womanhood...
Wisened by her walk in life, Wisened by her Path...
Answered the call.
And the fire heart, passion heart, of her deepest desire
and longing to be that which she was called to be...

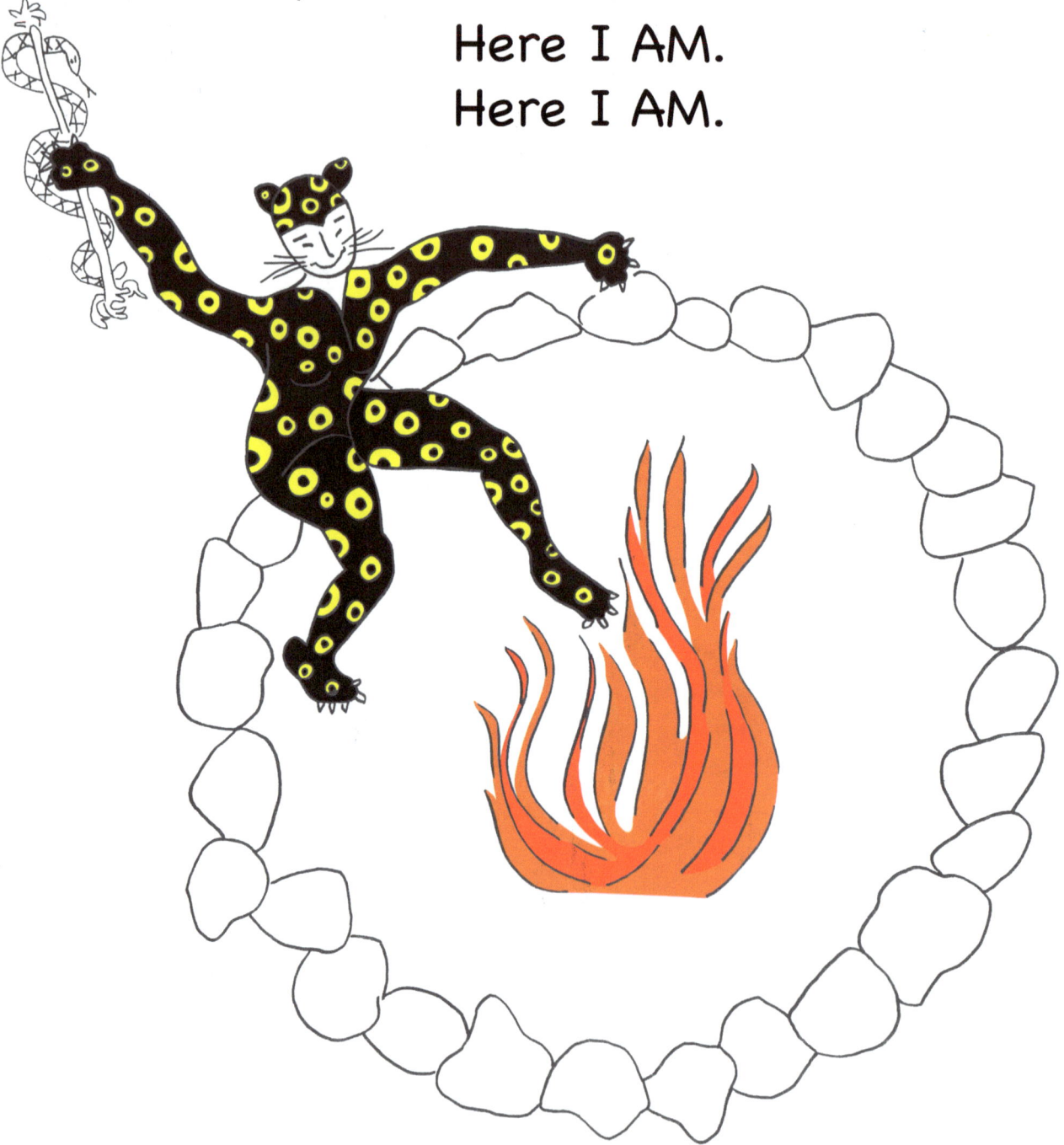

And she said,

Here I AM.
Here I AM.

I join the Circle now with bowed head.
I bring my gifts to the Circle as a blessing...
Ah-ah-ah...
Offering them back to Creator with tobacco,
With the smoke and fire and ritual of this calling...

This STEPPING INTO POWER.

I bow my head.
It is a sacred act.
I bow my head in awe and wonder,
I bow my head and bend my knee
    to Great Mother,
Great Mother Earth who supports and nourishes me,
Who gives me all that I need to BE.

I lift my eyes to Father Sky again...
To thank the Sky's spirit, And seeing the blue around me...

A feeling there are no limitations . . .
That all things are truly possible . . .
And within the realm of unlimited choices,

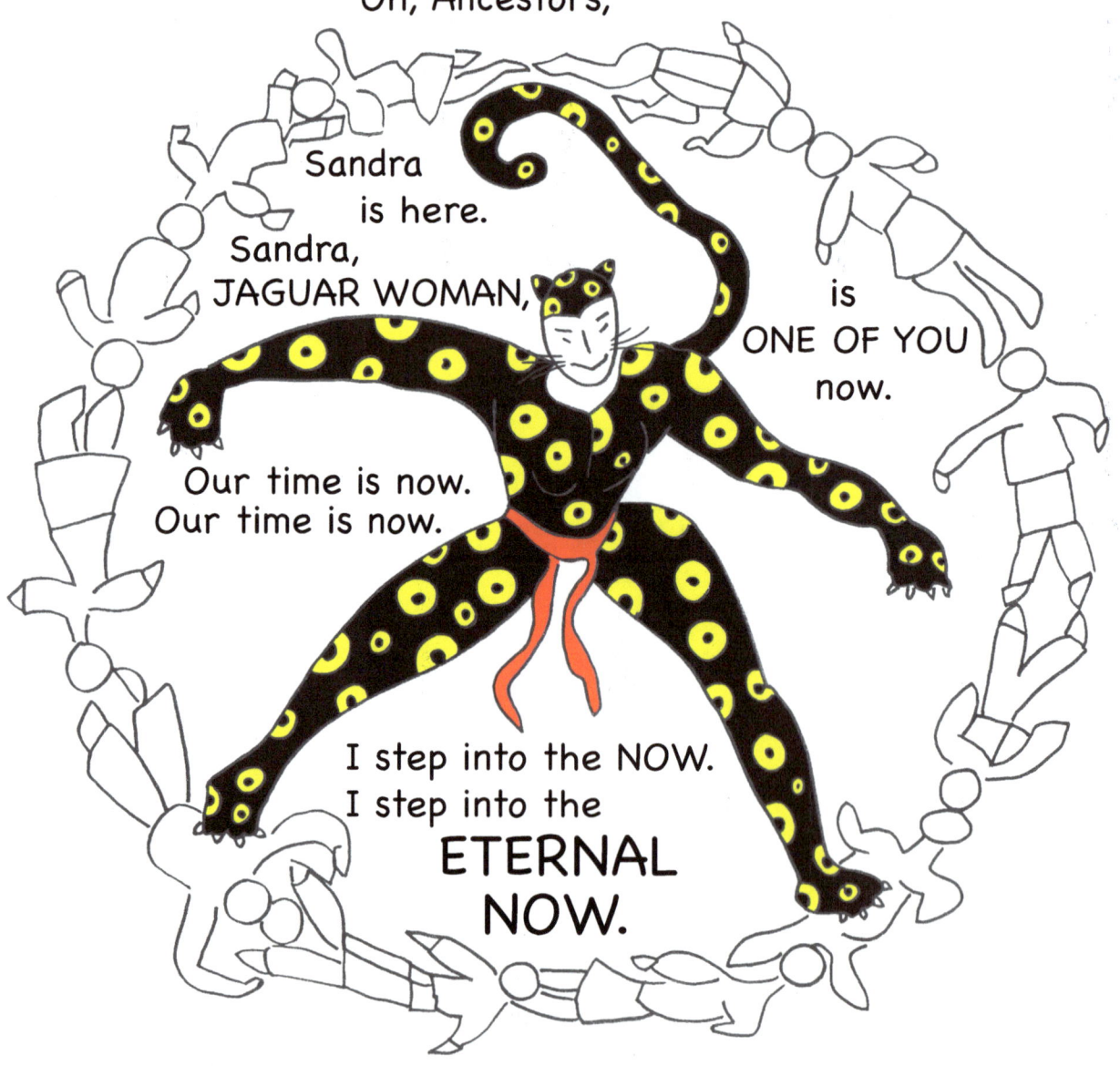

SANDRA'S JOURNEY QUESTIONS TO PONDER

1. What major obstacles have you encountered in your life? What has been or is your "dark night of the soul"?

    a. Have you lost a parent, child, loved one or favorite pet?
    b. Have you had to overcome an illness, injury, or handicap?
    c. Have you failed at a career or not succeeded at something you wanted to do?
    d. Has something you valued dearly been ruined or destroyed?

2. What was your emotional response to this loss? Were you afraid, hurt, or angry? How did you behave when this happened to you? What did you say and do?

3. How did you cope? How did you overcome this obstacle or get through this ordeal? Did you do this alone? Did other people help you? Did you enlist the aid of an animal totem or power animal? If so, how did you EMBODY this animal's attributes and/or strengths? Did you consult a higher power? If so, was this an external or internal source of power? What "symbolic form" did this power assume? Was it animal, plant, or mineral or human or superhuman? How did you access it or communicate with it?

4. Why do you think you were confronted with this challenge and/or obstacle? Was it an "accident"? Or do you think that there was a reason or higher purpose involved? How was the "little picture" of your life trying to inform you about the "bigger picture"? Are you able to look at your life in a symbolic way?

5. Did you learn anything from this experience? Did this experience change you for the better or for worse? Have you healed from this experience or do you still feel fragmented and wounded? Do you feel that you lost a part of yourself, a part of your Soul that you can never recover? Or have your accepted responsibility for your own healing? What have you done to heal yourself—to make yourself whole? Or are you still carrying this wound from your past into your present and future?

6. What were the "gifts" you received from this experience? Do you feel "called" to use these gifts to help or to be of service to other people? To the planet? To God? If so, how? Will this experience empower you to conquer or overcome future obstacles or problems? What about it will "transfer" to other life situations or circumstances?